NVIDIA

AND THE

AI BOOM

Why Nvidia Remains
Unmatched in the AI Revolution

Rayford R. Taylor

ABOUT THE AUTHOR

 Rayford R. Taylor is a technology analyst and writer with a deep passion for artificial intelligence, semiconductor innovation, and the future of computing. With years of experience studying the impact of AI on industries worldwide, he specializes in breaking down complex tech trends into clear, engaging insights for readers of all backgrounds.

Rayford's work explores the intersection of AI, business strategy, and the global economy, offering a sharp perspective on how companies like Nvidia, Microsoft, and Google are shaping the future. His research dives into AI-driven transformations, from chip manufacturing to enterprise adoption, making his books essential reading for tech enthusiasts, investors, and industry professionals alike.

When he's not writing, Rayford enjoys exploring advancements in machine learning, discussing AI's future with industry experts, and staying ahead of the latest breakthroughs in computing.

INTRODUCTION

THE POWERHOUSE OF AI

Nvidia has become one of the most important companies in the world. It started as a small business making computer graphics cards. Now, it is a leader in artificial intelligence (AI) chip manufacturing. The company's success shows how much AI is growing and changing how businesses and people use technology.

In 2024, Nvidia's profits more than doubled. It earned $74.3 billion, and its sales continued to rise. This growth proves that AI is not just a passing trend. It is becoming a major part of everyday life, from smart assistants to self-driving cars. But Nvidia's success is also a sign of something bigger. When the company does well, the entire tech industry benefits. When it struggles, other companies feel the impact. This connection makes Nvidia a key indicator of how the technology sector is doing.

This chapter will explore how Nvidia rose to power, why its performance affects the entire industry, and what its recent financial success means for the future of AI.

FROM GRAPHICS CARDS TO AI CHIPS

In 1993, three engineers, Jensen Huang, Chris Malachowsky, and Curtis Priem, founded Nvidia. They believed that computer graphics would play a major role in the future. Their first products were graphics processing units (GPUs) designed to improve video game visuals.

For years, Nvidia focused on making better GPUs for gamers. In 1999, the company introduced the GeForce 256, which was dubbed the first GPU in history. This chip was faster and more powerful than anything before it, helping Nvidia gain popularity among gamers and software developers.

Then, something unexpected happened. Scientists and researchers realized that Nvidia's GPUs could do more than render graphics. These chips could also perform complex calculations much faster than regular computer processors. By the early 2010s, researchers were using Nvidia GPUs to train AI models. This discovery changed the company's future.

Nvidia saw the potential and invested heavily in AI. It built new chips designed specifically for machine learning and deep learning, the core technologies behind AI. It also created software tools to help businesses and researchers use its hardware more effectively. This decision set Nvidia apart from its competitors.

Today, Nvidia's chips are used in nearly every major AI project. Companies like Google, Microsoft, Amazon, and Tesla rely on them to power AI-driven products and services. Whether chatbots, facial recognition, or self-driving cars, Nvidia's hardware plays a critical role.

WHY NVIDIA'S PERFORMANCE MATTERS

Nvidia's success is about more than just making money. It reflects the health of the entire tech industry. Investors, analysts, and business leaders closely watch Nvidia's earnings reports to understand where AI is heading.

One reason is that Nvidia supplies the chips that make AI possible. If AI companies spend a lot of money on Nvidia's products, it suggests that AI demand is strong. If they cut back, it could mean AI development is slowing down.

Another reason is Nvidia's influence on stock markets. When the company performs well, other tech stocks often rise, too. This is because Nvidia's growth signals general confidence in AI and technology. On the other hand, if Nvidia struggles, investors may worry that AI is overhyped or not as profitable as expected.

For example, when Nvidia announced its strong 2024 earnings, the stock prices of other major tech companies like Google, Meta, Microsoft, and Amazon increased. This reaction showed that investors saw Nvidia's success as a sign that AI was still a good investment.

Nvidia's performance also affects industries beyond tech. Many companies are currently using AI to enhance their goods and services. If AI development slows down, healthcare, finance, and manufacturing companies might face delays in adopting new AI tools.

Because of these connections, Nvidia's earnings are more than just numbers. They help shape the future of technology and business.

THE SIGNIFICANCE OF NVIDIA'S 2024 FINANCIAL SUCCESS

Nvidia's financial results for 2024 were staggering. The company's revenue for the year reached $74.3 billion, more than twice what it earned the previous year. In the last quarter alone, it made $39.3 billion in sales, a 78% increase from the same time in 2023.

Profits also soared. Nvidia made $22 billion in the final quarter of 2024, a 72% jump from the previous year. Few companies in history have achieved this level of growth in such a short time.

There are several reasons behind this massive success:

1. The AI Boom

Companies around the world are rushing to develop AI-powered products. Businesses need powerful chips to train and run AI models, from chatbots like ChatGPT to automated customer service tools. Nvidia is the leading supplier of these chips, giving it a huge advantage.

2. High Demand for AI Infrastructure

Tech giants like Microsoft, Google, and Meta spend billions on AI infrastructure. They need Nvidia's chips to build massive data centers that can handle AI workloads. Analysts say the top seven tech companies plan to invest $325 billion in AI-related projects in 2025.

3. Lack of Strong Competition

Although other companies like AMD and Intel make AI chips, Nvidia remains far ahead. Its GPUs are considered the best for AI training, and its software ecosystem, including CUDA and TensorRT, makes it even harder for competitors to catch up.

4. The Expanding Use of AI

AI is moving beyond traditional tech companies—industries like healthcare, finance, and automotive use AI to improve efficiency and reduce costs. Nvidia's CEO, Jensen Huang, predicts that even cars will be AI-powered in the future, constantly collecting data and improving their performance.

Challenges and Concerns

Despite its strong performance, Nvidia faces challenges. One major concern is competition from new AI models, such as DeepSeek. DeepSeek is a Chinese AI model that is more power-efficient than existing systems. Some experts worry that AI companies might not need as many Nvidia chips if they switch to more efficient models.

Another concern is the cost of AI development. Some investors fear companies spend too much on AI infrastructure without seeing immediate profits. If businesses decide to cut back on AI investments, Nvidia's sales could slow down.

There are also geopolitical risks. The U.S. government has placed restrictions on selling advanced AI chips to China, a major market for AI technology. These restrictions could limit Nvidia's growth in the region.

Despite these challenges, many analysts believe Nvidia's future remains bright. AI continues to expand into new industries, and demand for AI hardware is expected to stay strong.

Nvidia's rise from a graphics card company to an AI powerhouse is remarkable. It recognized the potential of AI early and positioned itself as the leading provider of AI chips. Its success reflects the growing role of AI in modern life.

The company's 2024 financial results confirm that AI development is still accelerating. Nvidia's performance is a key indicator of the tech industry's health. When it thrives, other companies benefit. When it struggles, the entire sector feels the impact.

While challenges exist, Nvidia remains at the center of AI innovation. Its influence may continue for years to come, and its influence on how AI develops in the future will only increase as the technology becomes more sophisticated and pervasive.

CHAPTER 2

THE AI GOLD RUSH—WHY NVIDIA REMAINS UNMATCHED

Artificial intelligence (AI) is changing the world. It powers everything from smart assistants to self-driving cars. But AI systems need a lot of computing power to work properly. This is where Nvidia comes in.

For artificial intelligence, Nvidia produces the most powerful graphics processing units, or GPUs. These chips help computers process huge amounts of data quickly. Companies like Google, Microsoft, Amazon, and Meta rely on Nvidia's hardware to run their AI models. Even with new competition, Nvidia remains the top choice for AI computing.

This chapter explains why Nvidia's GPUs are so important, how the company stays ahead, and how its success impacts the tech industry.

THE CRITICAL ROLE OF NVIDIA'S GPUS IN POWERING AI SYSTEMS

Artificial intelligence is built on machine learning. This process allows computers to recognize patterns, make predictions, and improve over time. But training an AI model takes a massive amount of calculations. A regular computer processor (CPU) is too slow for this job.

GPUs, however, are perfect for AI. Unlike CPUs, which handle one task at a time, GPUs process thousands of tasks at once. This ability makes them ideal for AI training, where computers must process millions of data points quickly.

Why AI Needs So Much Power

To understand why AI needs powerful GPUs, imagine training a chatbot. The AI must study billions of words from books, websites, and conversations. It must learn grammar, understand meaning, and generate human-like responses. This process requires extreme computing power.

A normal computer might take months to train a large AI model. With Nvidia's GPUs, the same task can be done in days or even hours. This speed is crucial for companies trying to improve AI quickly.

Nvidia's Advantage: Hardware and Software

Nvidia dominates AI computing because it doesn't just make hardware—it also provides software. The company created CUDA, a programming tool that allows AI developers to use GPUs efficiently. CUDA has become the industry standard, making it difficult for companies to switch to other chipmakers.

Beyond CUDA, Nvidia has developed special AI chips like the A100 and H100, which are optimized for deep learning. These chips are used in everything from language models like ChatGPT to image recognition systems.

Even as other companies try to compete, Nvidia's combination of powerful hardware and easy-to-use software gives it a huge advantage.

WHY NVIDIA'S DOMINANCE CONTINUES DESPITE INCREASED COMPETITION

Many companies are trying to compete with Nvidia, but none have been able to take its place. AMD and Intel make GPUs, but they struggle to match Nvidia's performance. New players, like Google and Amazon, are developing their own AI chips, yet they still rely on Nvidia for many projects.

Competitors' Challenges

AMD and Intel

- AMD has made progress with AI-focused GPUs, but its software tools aren't as popular as Nvidia's CUDA.
- Intel has focused more on traditional computer processors and has struggled to compete in the AI market.

Google's Tensor Processing Units (TPUs)

- Google has created TPUs, which are custom chips for AI. These chips perform well for Google's own projects, like search and cloud services.
- However, TPUs are not widely used outside Google, limiting their impact.

Amazon and Microsoft's Custom Chips

- Amazon and Microsoft have designed AI chips for their cloud services, but these chips mainly handle specific tasks rather than general AI training.

- Many AI startups and researchers still prefer Nvidia's GPUs because they work well with existing AI models.

Why Nvidia Still Leads

Even with these competitors, Nvidia remains the best choice for AI computing. Its GPUs are more powerful, its software is widely used, and its products are available to a broader audience.

AI companies need chips that work reliably and can handle the latest AI models. Nvidia has spent years perfecting its technology. Switching to another chipmaker would mean rewriting software, which is costly and time-consuming. Because of this, most AI companies stick with Nvidia.

MARKET REACTION TO NVIDIA'S SUCCESS

Nvidia's growth has been incredible. The company made $74.3 billion in 2024, more than double its earnings from the previous year. This success has had a huge impact on the stock market and the entire tech industry.

How Google, Meta, Microsoft, and Amazon Benefited

Big tech companies rely on AI to improve their products. When Nvidia succeeds, it means these companies have the tools they need to expand their AI services.

- **Google** uses AI in its search engine, YouTube recommendations, and cloud services. Nvidia's powerful chips help train Google's AI models faster, making its products better.

- **Meta** (formerly Facebook) uses AI to personalize news feeds, improve ad targeting, and develop virtual reality (VR) experiences. Nvidia's hardware helps process the massive amounts of data needed for these tasks.

- **Microsoft** has invested heavily in AI, including partnerships with OpenAI (the company behind ChatGPT). Microsoft's cloud service, Azure, offers AI computing powered by Nvidia's GPUs.

- **Amazon** uses AI for Alexa, its recommendation system, and its cloud services. Nvidia's chips help Amazon provide faster and smarter AI solutions for businesses.

When Nvidia reported record profits in 2024, these companies saw their stock prices rise. Investors saw Nvidia's success as a sign that AI spending would continue, benefiting the entire tech industry.

The Nasdaq's Response and Tech Stock Trends

The performance of technology stocks is monitored by the Nasdaq Composite Index. Nasdaq trends have been significantly influenced by Nvidia's success.

- **Stock Market Influence:** When Nvidia's earnings reports show strong growth, investor confidence in tech stocks rises. This often leads to increases in stock prices for other AI-focused companies.

- **AI Investment Boom:** Many investors are betting that AI will drive future profits. As a result, they invest in companies that depend on AI, such as cloud computing firms and AI software developers.

- **Short-Term Volatility:** While Nvidia's long-term growth has been strong, its stock price has seen ups and downs. Some investors worry that AI spending could slow down, leading to short-term declines. However, overall confidence in AI remains high.

In early 2025, the Nasdaq saw a small drop, partly due to concerns about new AI competition from DeepSeek, a Chinese AI model. However, Nvidia's strong earnings reassured investors, and tech stocks rebounded.

THE FUTURE OF NVIDIA'S AI DOMINANCE

Nvidia's position in the AI market remains strong, but the future holds challenges and opportunities.

Continued Demand for AI Chips

AI is expanding beyond tech companies. Industries like healthcare, finance, and automotive are using AI to improve efficiency and decision-making. Nvidia's GPUs will continue to be in high demand as businesses adopt AI-powered tools.

Advancements in AI Hardware

Nvidia is working on its next generation of AI chips, such as the Blackwell series. These chips promise even faster performance and better energy efficiency. As AI models become more advanced, the need for more powerful hardware will grow.

Challenges from New AI Models

The rise of AI models like DeepSeek has raised questions about AI efficiency. Some experts believe that AI models will become less reliant on Nvidia's GPUs if they can run on simpler hardware. However, Nvidia is also investing in AI efficiency, ensuring that its products remain essential.

Regulatory and Geopolitical Risks

Nvidia faces restrictions on selling its most advanced chips to China due to U.S. government policies. Since China is a major market for AI technology, these restrictions could impact future sales. However, Nvidia is working on alternative products that meet regulatory requirements while still serving international customers.

Nvidia's role in AI is unmatched. Its GPUs power the most advanced AI systems, and its software tools make it easy for companies to develop AI applications. Despite growing competition, Nvidia remains the preferred choice for AI computing.

The company's financial success has boosted confidence in AI investment. Major tech companies like Google, Meta, Microsoft, and Amazon continue to benefit from Nvidia's innovations. The stock market reacts strongly to Nvidia's performance, making it a key player in the tech industry.

While challenges exist, Nvidia's strong position suggests it will continue to lead AI development. As AI spreads into new industries, Nvidia's impact will only grow.

CHAPTER 3

THE THREAT TO NVIDIA'S DOMINATION FROM DEEPSEEK

For many years, Nvidia has dominated the AI chip market. Globally, artificial intelligence systems are fueled by powerful GPUs. Nvidia powers the AI models of tech behemoths like Amazon, Microsoft, Meta, and Google. However, DeepSeek, a new player, appeared in 2024.

A Chinese startup created the sophisticated AI model known as DeepSeek. DeepSeek is intended to be more effective than many current AI systems. It uses less processing power while delivering powerful performance. This breakthrough has raised serious questions for Nvidia and the broader AI industry.

Businesses might require fewer powerful chips if AI models improve efficiency, and investors are uneasy about this. Some people wonder if tech firms are overspending on AI infrastructure, and others wonder if Nvidia's dominance could weaken in the future.

This chapter covers the impact of DeepSeek, the controversy surrounding AI spending, and the potential dangers Nvidia faces as AI technology advances.

DEEPSEEK'S DEVELOPMENT AS A REVOLUTIONARY AI MODEL

In 2024, a Chinese startup created DeepSeek. Because of its effectiveness, it attracted attention right away. DeepSeek produces excellent results with fewer resources than AI models, which typically require enormous processing power.

Why DeepSeek Stands out

Lower Consumption of Power

- To function, the majority of AI systems require thousands of Nvidia GPUs. On the other hand, DeepSeek uses fewer chips to function effectively.
- This implies that businesses could depend less on pricey hardware.

Cost Savings

- AI firms invest billions of dollars in data centers and cloud computing. DeepSeek's effectiveness may reduce these expenses.
- This might open up AI to more companies than just technological giants.

Pressure from the Competition on Nvidia

- AI developers might purchase less Nvidia hardware if they accomplish the same goals with fewer GPUs.

- Over time, this change may result in less demand for Nvidia's chips.

The introduction of DeepSeek has compelled businesses to reevaluate their AI strategies. Even though Nvidia is still the best option for AI hardware, some analysts think the market may shift to more effective models like DeepSeek.

WHY INVESTORS ARE CONCERNED ABOUT DEEPSEEK'S EFFICIENCY

The strong demand for AI chips is essential to Nvidia's success. Nvidia's revenue increases as more businesses require its hardware. However, DeepSeek's effectiveness might alter that.

Businesses might not require as many Nvidia GPUs if AI models improve their understanding of how to use processing power. As a result, Nvidia's sales would decline, and its growth would be slowed.

Reactions of the Stock Market

Following the announcement of DeepSeek, Nvidia's stock price dropped 5%. Investors were concerned that spending on AI might decline. Many had anticipated that AI companies would keep purchasing chips at the same accelerated rate. DeepSeek disputed that notion.

Many tech companies are included in the Nasdaq Composite Index, which also saw a slight decline. This demonstrated that investors were keeping a careful eye on AI spending. Other AI-related businesses may also be impacted if Nvidia's earnings drop.

The Reaction of Tech Companies

Despite the concerns, large tech companies have kept investing in AI. Amazon, Microsoft, Google, and Meta still see AI as essential to their future. They still purchase Nvidia's chips even as they investigate more effective AI models.

According to renowned analyst Dan Ives, large tech firms intend to invest $325 billion in AI infrastructure by 2025. No business wants to lag in AI development, he said. AI businesses still require a lot of processing power, even if DeepSeek lowers power requirements.

For now, DeepSeek has not slowed AI spending. Investors, however, are cautious about whether this will change in the future.

THE DEBATE OVER AI SPENDING

The largest technological investment in recent years has been in artificial intelligence. Businesses have invested billions to create AI-powered goods. However, some analysts wonder if this spending can continue.

Do Tech Companies Invest Too Much in AI Infrastructure?

Tech companies are racing to develop better AI systems. This competition has fueled massive expenditures in cloud computing, data centers, and GPUs, which has helped Nvidia.

Some analysts, however, are concerned that businesses are spending excessively quickly.

- **Training AI models are costly**. Training a large AI system can cost hundreds of millions of dollars.

- **Computing power is limited:** Even with powerful chips, AI companies must deal with space and energy limitations.

- **Uncertainty surrounds returns on investment:** Despite its excitement, businesses have not yet fully monetized many AI projects.

The effectiveness of DeepSeek has fueled this discussion. Why invest so much in infrastructure if AI models can produce comparable outcomes using fewer resources?

Defending AI Investments

The majority of tech executives think AI spending is essential despite reservations. According to Jensen Huang, CEO of Nvidia, artificial intelligence will revolutionize almost every sector. He cites automation, medical research, and self-driving cars as areas where AI will be extremely valuable.

Huang thinks that the demand for Nvidia's chips will rise as AI becomes more efficient. As AI becomes more affordable to operate, more companies will use it, which might broaden Nvidia's clientele beyond major IT firms.

Some experts concur. They claim that although AI models will improve, sophisticated chips will still be needed. AI will continue to require high-performance hardware even if DeepSeek lowers power requirements.

POSSIBLE RISKS TO NVIDIA'S LONG-TERM DEVELOPMENT

Although Nvidia is still at the forefront of AI computing, the company will face difficulties in the future.

1. Other AI Chipmakers' Competition

Nvidia's sustained dominance has come under scrutiny due to DeepSeek. Although rivals are developing alternatives, Nvidia remains the leading supplier of AI hardware.

- Tensor Processing Units (TPUs), created by Google, are the brains behind its AI services.
- To increase cloud computing efficiency, Amazon has developed its own AI chips.
- To compete with Nvidia, AMD and Intel are spending money on GPUs with an AI focus.

None of these businesses has surpassed Nvidia thus far. However, as AI becomes more efficient, businesses might consider alternative hardware choices.

2. Difficulties with Regulation

The government also imposes restrictions on Nvidia. For example, the United States has restricted the sale of cutting-edge AI chips to China. These limitations may affect Nvidia's earnings because China is a significant AI market.

Nvidia has responded by developing chips modified to comply with U.S. export regulations. However, if trade tensions worsen, Nvidia's capacity to sell AI hardware internationally may be impacted.

3. The Transition to More Effective AI Models

DeepSeek has demonstrated that AI can be tuned to consume less power. If this trend persists, businesses may become less dependent on high-performance GPUs.

In response, Nvidia has already increased the effectiveness of its AI. The business is developing new chip designs that use less energy and provide better performance. If it can maintain its efficiency lead, Nvidia may be able to stop a drop in demand.

DeepSeek has sparked an important discussion in the AI industry. It has demonstrated that AI can be more effective, which begs the question of how much processing power businesses require.

Nvidia continues to be the industry leader in the production of AI chips. AI spending is rising, and tech giants are purchasing its GPUs. But the industry is evolving. The need for Nvidia's high-performance chips may eventually decline as AI models become more effective.

Investors are listening carefully. Nvidia's growth might slow if businesses move toward less-power AI models. Nvidia is simultaneously trying to maintain its lead by increasing the effectiveness of its own AI.

The race to develop AI is far from over. Nvidia, DeepSeek, and other rivals will keep pushing the envelope of what is conceivable. The future of AI will depend on how the sector responds to efficiency gains.

CHAPTER 4

THE MARKET'S REACTION— JITTERS AND CONFIDENCE

Nvidia has seen remarkable growth, fueled by rising demand for artificial intelligence (AI). The company's powerful GPUs drive AI systems worldwide, making it a key player in the tech industry. But even as Nvidia sets record profits, its stock has seen ups and downs.

In early 2025, Nvidia's stock dropped by 5%, causing some investors to worry. Yet, over the past year, the stock had still climbed 65%, showing strong overall growth. Some experts fear that AI infrastructure costs are getting too high, while others believe that more efficient AI models will boost Nvidia's future.

This chapter explores Nvidia's stock trends, investor concerns, and the debate over whether AI's growing efficiency will help or hurt Nvidia.

NVIDIA'S STOCK TRENDS: A STORY OF GROWTH AND DIPS

The stock market is always changing. Even the most successful companies see their share prices rise and fall. Nvidia is no exception.

The 5% Decline in Early 2025

At the start of 2025, Nvidia's stock took a hit, falling by 5%. Several factors contributed to this decline:

DeepSeek's AI Model

- A Chinese startup, DeepSeek, introduced an AI model that uses less computing power than existing systems.

- Some investors worried that if AI companies switched to less power-hungry models, demand for Nvidia's GPUs might drop.

Concerns About AI Spending

- Investors questioned whether tech giants like Google, Microsoft, and Meta were spending too much on AI infrastructure.
- If these companies decided to slow down their AI investments, Nvidia's revenue could take a hit.

Overall Tech Market Weakness

- The broader tech market wasn't doing well in early 2025. The Nasdaq Composite, a stock index focused on tech companies, had also dropped by 1%.
- When tech stocks fall, Nvidia often follows since it is one of the biggest tech companies.

Despite these short-term worries, Nvidia's long-term growth remained strong.

A 65% Year-Over-Year Stock Growth

Even with its early 2025 dip, Nvidia's stock had climbed an impressive 65% over the past year. That's because the company continued to dominate the AI chip market.

Several factors drove this massive growth:

Explosive AI Demand

- Companies everywhere are racing to build AI-powered products.
- Nvidia's GPUs remain the best choice for training and running AI models.

Record Profits

- Nvidia more than doubled its yearly profits 2024, reaching $74.3 billion.
- Investors tend to buy stocks from companies with strong earnings, which helped boost Nvidia's value.

Big Tech Partnerships

- Nvidia supplies AI chips to major players like Microsoft, Google, Amazon, and Meta.
- These companies continue to invest billions in AI, keeping Nvidia's business strong.

Overall, Nvidia's long-term growth outweighed short-term fears.

INVESTOR CONCERNS ABOUT AI INFRASTRUCTURE COSTS

Even though Nvidia has been successful, some investors worry that AI is getting too expensive. Training AI models require massive energy and computing power, leading to high costs.

The Rising Cost of AI Training

AI models have become more complex over time. The latest systems, like OpenAI's GPT-4 and Google's Gemini, need enormous data centers full of high-performance GPUs to function. Running these models costs companies millions, if not billions, of dollars.

For example:

- OpenAI reportedly spent over $100 million training a single version of GPT-4.
- Google and Meta are investing billions in AI-focused data centers.
- Even startups trying to compete in AI must raise huge amounts of money to afford Nvidia's chips.

Some investors fear that these costs could slow down AI adoption. If companies find AI too expensive to sustain, they might spend less on Nvidia's products.

Pressure to Justify AI Spending

Tech companies are pressured to show that AI investments will lead to profits. While AI chatbots and image generators are exciting, many businesses are still learning how to profit from them.

If AI companies struggle to turn a profit, they may:

- Reduce their spending on Nvidia's chips.
- Shift towards cheaper computing alternatives.
- Focus on making AI more efficient to cut costs.

Investors are closely watching how AI firms balance spending and revenue.

WHY SOME EXPERTS BELIEVE EFFICIENT AI MODELS COULD ACCELERATE ADOPTION

Not everyone sees high AI costs as a problem. Some experts believe that making AI more efficient will help Nvidia in the long run.

How AI Efficiency Benefits Nvidia

Faster AI Adoption

- If AI models become cheaper to train and run, more businesses will use AI.

- This could lead to an even bigger demand for Nvidia's AI chips.

More AI Use in Different Industries

- Right now, AI is mostly used by big tech companies.
- If AI becomes more affordable, smaller companies, hospitals, banks, and other industries might start using AI, increasing demand for Nvidia's products.

Ongoing Need for Powerful Hardware

- Even if AI becomes more efficient, it will still need high-performance chips.
- Nvidia continues to release more powerful GPUs, ensuring its relevance in the AI market.

In this view, better AI efficiency could fuel Nvidia's growth, not slow it down.

DeepSeek's AI Model: A Threat or an Opportunity?

DeepSeek's AI model sparked discussions about AI efficiency. Some investors saw it as a threat to Nvidia, but others believe it could lead to more AI adoption.

DeepSeek's model uses less computing power, which could:

- Reduce costs for companies using AI.
- Encourage more businesses to experiment with AI.
- Lead to even greater demand for Nvidia's GPUs as AI expands to more industries.

While some fear DeepSeek could hurt Nvidia, others argue that any improvement in AI efficiency will only expand the market, benefiting Nvidia in the long term.

BALANCING JITTERS AND CONFIDENCE

Emotions often drive stock market movements. Investors react to news, predictions, and short-term changes, even when a company's long-term potential remains strong.

Why Nvidia's Future Still Looks Bright

Despite concerns about AI costs and competition, Nvidia's position in the market remains strong for several reasons:

It's Still the Industry Leader

- Nvidia's GPUs power the majority of AI systems.
- Competitors like AMD and Intel are still far behind in AI computing.

Tech Giants Are Still Spending on AI

- Microsoft, Google, and Amazon continue to invest heavily in AI infrastructure.
- These companies need Nvidia's chips to power their AI services.

AI Is Still Growing

- AI is not just a trend—it's becoming an essential part of business and technology.
- As more industries adopt AI, demand for Nvidia's products will likely continue to rise.

While short-term jitters may cause temporary stock dips, Nvidia's long-term outlook remains strong.

What Investors Should Watch For

As Nvidia moves forward, investors will be watching several key factors:

- **AI Spending Trends:** Will companies keep investing billions in AI infrastructure?

- **Competition:** Will new AI chips from companies like Google and AMD impact Nvidia's sales?

- **New AI Models:** Will more efficient AI models help or hurt Nvidia?

Nvidia's stock has seen ups and downs, but its long-term growth remains strong. A 5% dip in early 2025 worried some investors, but the company's stock was still up 65% over the past year.

Investor concerns about high AI infrastructure costs have sparked debate. Some fear companies will spend less on AI, while others believe more efficient AI models will drive even greater adoption.

Despite market jitters, Nvidia continues to dominate AI computing. As AI becomes more widespread, Nvidia's role in the industry will likely remain secure.

CHAPTER 5

BIG TECH'S AI INVESTMENT—THE $325 BILLION BET

Artificial intelligence is the future of technology. It's changing how people work, shop, communicate, and drive. Companies are racing to build smarter AI systems, which require a lot of computing power.

The biggest tech companies—often called the "Magnificent Seven"—are leading this charge. Microsoft, Amazon, Meta, Apple, Alphabet, Nvidia, and Tesla are investing billions in AI. Their combined spending on AI infrastructure is expected to reach $325 billion in 2025.

This chapter explores how these companies spend their money, why they continue to rely on Nvidia, and how competition from DeepSeek is affecting the AI race.

CAPITAL EXPENDITURES FROM THE "MAGNIFICENT SEVEN"

Capital expenditures (CapEx) refer to money spent on physical assets like data centers, supercomputers, and AI research. Large tech firms are investing heavily in AI because they think it will boost profits in the future.

AI models require massive data centers filled with powerful chips to process information. These data centers need specialized cooling systems because they produce heat and use massive amounts of electricity. Every company in the Magnificent Seven is racing to expand its AI infrastructure.

Microsoft

Microsoft is one of the biggest investors in AI. The company has partnered with OpenAI, the creator of ChatGPT, to bring AI-powered tools to businesses and consumers.

- **Investment in AI Data Centers:** Microsoft is spending tens of billions to build AI supercomputers for OpenAI.
- **Azure AI Services:** Microsoft's cloud platform, Azure, offers AI computing power to companies worldwide. Many businesses rely on Azure to train AI models.
- **AI in Software:** Microsoft has added AI features to products like Office 365, Windows, and GitHub Copilot to help users work faster.

Amazon

Amazon incorporates AI into everything from product recommendations to its Alexa voice assistant. but in artificial intelligence, its investing goes to the world's largest cloud computing company(AWS).

- **AWS AI Services:** Amazon's cloud platform offers AI tools to businesses, helping them build smarter applications.
- **Custom AI Chips:** Amazon is developing its AI processors, such as the Trainium and Inferentia chips. However, many AWS customers still prefer Nvidia's GPUs for AI training.
- **AI in Logistics:** Amazon uses AI to optimize warehouse operations, delivery routes, and supply chain management.

Meta (Facebook)

Meta invests heavily in AI to improve its social media platforms and build the metaverse—a virtual reality world where people can interact online.

- **AI-Powered Content:** Meta uses AI to recommend posts, detect harmful content, and improve ad targeting.

- **AI for Virtual Reality (VR) and Augmented Reality (AR):** AI plays a key role in making VR and AR experiences more realistic.

- **AI Infrastructure:** Meta is building massive data centers with Nvidia GPUs to power its AI research.

Apple

Apple keeps its AI projects more secretive than other tech giants, but it's making major investments in AI-driven products.

- **AI in iPhones and Macs:** Apple is developing on-device AI, meaning AI features run directly on iPhones, iPads, and Macs without relying on cloud computing.

- **Siri and Voice AI:** Apple is improving its Siri assistant with better AI understanding.

- **AI for Health and Security:** AI powers Apple's health-tracking features and enhances privacy protections.

Alphabet (Google's Parent Company)

Google has been a leader in AI for years. Its AI research lab, DeepMind, has made groundbreaking discoveries in machine learning.

- **Google Search and AI:** AI helps Google provide better search results, smarter ads, and more relevant YouTube recommendations.
- **AI in Google Cloud:** Like Microsoft and Amazon, Google is offering AI computing services through Google Cloud.
- **TPUs (Tensor Processing Units):** Google has developed AI chips, but many companies still use Nvidia's GPUs.

Nvidia

Unlike the other six companies, Nvidia doesn't provide AI services directly to consumers. Instead, it supplies the chips that power AI for everyone else.

- **AI Superchips:** Nvidia's A100 and H100 GPUs are the backbone of AI computing. Companies worldwide rely on them to train machine learning models.

- **Software and AI Research:** Nvidia also develops AI software, such as CUDA, making AI models easier to program.

- **Expansion into New Industries:** Nvidia's chips are used in everything from self-driving cars to medical research.

Tesla

Tesla is best known for electric cars but is also an AI-driven company.

- **Full Self-Driving (FSD):** Tesla uses AI to improve its autonomous driving software. The more Tesla cars drive, the more data the AI collects to make driving safer.

- **Supercomputers for AI Training:** Tesla is building an AI supercomputer called Dojo to process vast amounts of driving data.

- **AI Robots:** Tesla is developing humanoid robots that could assist in factories and homes.

WHY DEMAND FOR NVIDIA'S CHIPS REMAINS STRONG DESPITE DEEPSEEK

DeepSeek, a Chinese AI startup, recently introduced a more efficient AI model. Some experts believe this could lower the demand for Nvidia's GPUs. However, Nvidia's chips remain essential for AI development.

DeepSeek's Efficiency vs. Nvidia's Power

DeepSeek's AI model is designed to be more energy-efficient. It requires less computing power than traditional AI models. This means some companies might spend less on expensive GPUs.

But DeepSeek doesn't eliminate the need for high-performance AI chips. Advanced AI models, like those used in self-driving cars, medical research, and robotics, still require maximum computing power. Nvidia's GPUs are the best at handling these demanding tasks.

Tech Giants Aren't Slowing Down AI Spending

Despite concerns over DeepSeek, major tech companies continue investing billions in AI infrastructure. Wedbush analyst Dan Ives estimates that the Magnificent Seven will spend $325 billion in 2025 alone.

This spending covers:

- Expanding AI data centers
- Buying more Nvidia GPUs
- Developing custom AI software
- Hiring top AI researchers

The DeepSeek situation hasn't changed their long-term strategy. AI remains their top priority, and they will spend whatever it takes to stay ahead.

"No One Wants to Lose Their Place in Line"

AI companies are rushing to secure Nvidia's next-generation Blackwell chips, which will be even more powerful than the current H100 models.

Analysts say no major AI company has canceled or slowed down their GPU orders due to DeepSeek. Instead, businesses are worried about falling behind. Since Nvidia's chips are in high demand, companies fear that they might struggle to get enough supply if they don't buy them now.

LOOKING AHEAD: THE FUTURE OF AI INVESTMENT

The AI boom is just getting started. As more companies integrate AI into their businesses, the demand for AI chips and computing power will keep growing.

Industries Expanding AI Use

AI is spreading beyond big tech. Industries like healthcare, finance, and manufacturing are investing in AI to improve efficiency. Nvidia's GPUs will continue to play a major role in these sectors.

Energy and Sustainability Challenges

AI requires massive amounts of electricity. Some companies are looking for ways to make AI computing more energy-efficient. Nvidia is developing lower-power AI chips, but achieving the right balance of performance and efficiency is difficult.

Regulatory and Political Risks

Governments around the world are paying closer attention to AI. New laws and regulations could affect how companies invest in AI. Export restrictions on AI chips, especially to China, could impact Nvidia's business.

The Bottom Line

Despite these challenges, the AI race is far from over. Big tech companies are betting huge amounts of money on AI because they see it as the future of their business. Nvidia remains at the center of this revolution, supplying the chips that power the world's most advanced AI systems.

Even as new AI models like DeepSeek emerge, Nvidia's dominance in AI hardware remains unshaken. For now, tech giants are all-in on AI, and their $325 billion bet shows how much they believe in its future.

CHAPTER 6

NVIDIA'S ROLE IN THE FUTURE OF AI

Artificial intelligence is increasingly prevalent in daily life. It's transforming sectors like healthcare, finance, and even transportation, so it's no longer just for tech companies. A major contributor to this change is Nvidia, the industry leader in the production of AI chips.

Jensen Huang, the CEO, has a big idea for AI. He believes AI will power everything from self-driving cars to intelligent assistants in the workplace.

Nvidia's next-generation **Blackwell chips** are anticipated to advance AI even further, increasing its speed and effectiveness.

This chapter explores Huang's vision, how AI is expanding beyond tech, and why Nvidia will continue to shape the future of AI.

JENSEN HUANG'S AI VISION

Jensen Huang is a strong supporter of artificial intelligence. Under his direction, Nvidia transformed from a graphics card manufacturer to the most significant supplier of AI hardware globally.

Huang has recently outlined a future in which artificial intelligence will permeate every aspect of life. He thinks:

- AI will be used by businesses outside of the tech sector as well.
- Instead of replacing workers, AI will increase their productivity.

- AI-powered devices will gather and process Large volumes of data, enhancing decision-making.

His predictions regarding self-driving cars are among his most notable. According to Huang, there will be a billion AI-powered vehicles on the road in the future. These cars will do more than drive themselves; they will gather information, get better with time, and even interact with other artificial intelligence systems.

Additionally, he believes AI will play a significant role in corporate operations. Businesses will use AI to save time and make better decisions, from AI-powered customer support representatives to AI-driven financial analysis.

AI'S INTEGRATION INTO INDUSTRIES BEYOND TECH

AI isn't limited to Silicon Valley anymore. Businesses, healthcare providers, and automotive companies are currently using AI in ways that were not feasible only a few years ago.

Automotive: The Emergence of Data-Collecting, AI-Powered Automobiles

The development of self-driving technology has been ongoing for many years. Businesses that have significantly invested in autonomous vehicles include Tesla, Waymo, and General Motors. However, according to Jensen Huang, autonomous vehicles are only one aspect of artificial intelligence's potential in transportation.

AI-powered cars will collect data in addition to driving themselves.

- Sensors and cameras will be installed in every AI-powered vehicle to collect data on weather, traffic, and roads.
- Cloud servers will receive this data, and artificial intelligence (AI) systems will evaluate it to enhance navigation.

- Based on actual driving data, AI-powered cars will eventually get more innovative and safer.

Major automakers are already partnering with Nvidia to supply AI chips for smart cars and self-driving systems. The company's Drive platform allows cars to make better decisions while driving by processing large amounts of data in real-time.

Even cars that aren't entirely autonomous will still use AI for:

- Lane-keeping and collision avoidance are examples of driver assistance features.
- Voice-activated entertainment and navigation controls.
- Improvements in electric vehicles' energy efficiency.

AI-powered vehicles will proliferate over the next ten years. Nvidia's GPUs are the brains behind many of these cutting-edge systems so that they will play a critical role in this transition.

Business: Artificial Intelligence Boosting Output

 AI is also changing the workplace. Many businesses are using AI agents or software applications that carry out tasks automatically to increase productivity.

AI is utilized in:

- **Customer service:** AI chatbots provide prompt answers to consumer inquiries.
- **Marketing:** AI examines customer behavior to recommend more effective tactics.
- **Finance:** AI forecasts market trends, handles investments, and identifies fraud.

However, AI is progressing beyond basic tasks. AI may eventually serve as employees' full-time helper, assisting with:

- Composing emails and reports
- Summarizing long documents
- Analyzing complex data sets

According to Jensen Huang, AI will increase workers' productivity rather than replace them. Employees can concentrate on more crucial work while AI takes care of the repetitive tasks, saving them time.

Businesses that use AI-powered helpers could:

- Reduce the need for human labor on easy jobs to **save money.**
- **Make fewer mistakes** since AI doesn't suffer from fatigue or distractions.
- **Increase output** so that workers can complete more tasks in less time.

Nvidia already offers the software and hardware required for these AI assistants. Nvidia's contribution to powering these systems will only increase as AI becomes more prevalent in business.

NVIDIA'S BLACKWELL CHIPS' POTENTIAL AND UPCOMING DEVELOPMENTS

With the size growth of AI models, they require stronger hardware to function effectively. The upcoming Blackwell chips from Nvidia are anticipated to represent a significant advancement.

Why Is Blackwell Unique?

- **Faster AI Training:** Before AI models can be used, they must be trained. Blackwell chips will speed up and lower the cost of AI development by cutting down on training time.

- **Reduced Power Consumption:** AI processing uses a lot of energy. Thanks to Blackwell chips' increased energy efficiency, data centers will save money.

- **Improved Business Performance:** Blackwell's advancements will help businesses use AI for financial forecasting, medical analysis, and speech recognition.

According to experts, Blackwell chips will:

- **Maintain Nvidia's lead over rivals**, including fresh startups developing AI chips.
- **Make AI more widely available** so that smaller businesses can use it.
- Encourage AI to be **used in new fields** like robotics and space travel.

Beyond Blackwell: AI Hardware's Future

Nvidia is already developing even more sophisticated AI processors, even though Blackwell chips represent a significant advancement.

The following could be some of the upcoming significant innovations:

- **Quantum AI Chips:** These chips could process information thousands of times faster than today's GPUs.

- **AI-Optimized Data Centers:** Nvidia is creating supercomputers with AI research in mind.

- **Personal AI Devices:** Wearable AI chips that function as personal assistants may become commonplace in the future.

As Jensen Huang alluded to, Nvidia's long-term objective is to make AI computing as ubiquitous as electricity, the technology that drives everything in our environment.

CHAPTER 7

NVIDIA'S COMPETITIVE EDGE—WHY IT STILL LEADS AI HARDWARE

Nvidia dominates the AI hardware market because its chips are powerful, efficient, and widely used in machine learning. The company has spent years building a system that others struggle to match. From the H100 GPU to the upcoming Blackwell chip, Nvidia stays ahead by improving its technology and ensuring its software works seamlessly with its hardware.

H100 GPUS AND THEIR DOMINANCE IN AI TRAINING

AI systems need massive computing power. Training a large AI model like ChatGPT, requires thousands of GPUs running at full speed. Nvidia's H100 chip has become the top choice for this kind of work.

The H100, launched in 2022, is built on Nvidia's Hopper architecture. It improves speed, efficiency, and memory handling compared to earlier chips. One key feature is its Transformer Engine, which speeds up AI model training. This feature makes a considerable difference since AI models rely heavily on transformer-based architectures. It allows data to move faster through the chip, reducing the time needed to train AI.

Another reason the H100 dominates is its high-bandwidth memory (HBM). AI training requires moving massive amounts of data quickly. If a chip has slow memory, the entire training process slows down.

The H100's HBM allows models to process large amounts of information quickly.

Cloud providers like Amazon Web Services (AWS), Microsoft Azure, and Google Cloud offer H100 instances because they are the industry standard. Companies training AI models rely on these chips. While other chips exist, most AI developers prefer Nvidia because their software is built to work with it.

THE UPCOMING BLACKWELL CHIP AND ITS EXPECTED IMPACT

Nvidia is not stopping with the H100. The company is working on its next major chip, Blackwell, which is expected to launch in 2025. While details are still emerging, Blackwell will likely bring significant improvements.

One primary focus is power efficiency. AI training consumes massive amounts of electricity. Data centers running thousands of GPUs can use as much power as a small city. Nvidia knows that reducing energy use is crucial. Blackwell is expected to deliver more performance while using less electricity.

Blackwell may also improve multi-GPU communication. Many AI models are too large for a single GPU, so companies link multiple chips. If communication between GPUs is slow, training speed suffers. Nvidia has been working on technologies that improve how GPUs share data. Faster communication means models can train in less time, saving companies money.

Another key upgrade could be in AI inference. Training AI is only part of the equation. Once trained, models must run efficiently when users interact with them. Blackwell may include features that make AI models faster and cheaper to use. This is important for companies that run AI-powered services, from chatbots to image generators.

If Nvidia delivers on these improvements, Blackwell could strengthen its grip on the AI market. Competitors are racing to catch up, but Nvidia's track record suggests it will stay ahead.

WHY COMPETITORS STRUGGLE TO MATCH NVIDIA'S HARDWARE AND SOFTWARE INTEGRATION

Many companies have tried to challenge Nvidia. Intel, AMD, and Google have all developed AI chips. While some of these chips are powerful, they struggle to gain market share. The biggest reason is that Nvidia controls both hardware and software.

Most AI developers use CUDA (Compute Unified Device Architecture), Nvidia's programming platform for GPUs. CUDA has been around since 2006 and is deeply embedded in AI research. Developers have spent years building software that works with CUDA. This creates a lock-in effect—switching to another brand becomes difficult once companies start using Nvidia chips.

AMD and Intel offer alternative chips, but their software tools are less mature. Even if a competitor releases a GPU just as fast as Nvidia's, companies may hesitate to switch because their existing code is optimized for CUDA. Adapting software to a new platform is time-consuming and expensive.

Google has its Tensor Processing Units (TPUs), which are used for AI tasks inside Google's cloud services. While TPUs are powerful, they are not available for general use like Nvidia's chips. This limits their appeal to companies that need flexible AI hardware.

Another challenge for competitors is Nvidia's supply chain and partnerships. The company has strong relationships with major AI developers and cloud providers. When OpenAI, Meta, or Microsoft need AI chips, they first turn to Nvidia. Competing companies must fight to gain recognition in a market where Nvidia is the default choice.

THE ROLE OF CUDA IN CEMENTING NVIDIA'S MONOPOLY ON AI COMPUTING

CUDA is one of the biggest reasons Nvidia maintains its lead. It allows developers to program GPUs efficiently and is widely supported across industries.

Most AI frameworks, including TensorFlow and PyTorch, are optimized for CUDA. This means that developers writing AI code naturally rely on Nvidia's software. If a company wanted to switch to a non-Nvidia chip, it would need to rewrite or adapt large portions of its code. This is a significant barrier to entry for competitors.

CUDA also provides tools for optimizing AI workloads. It helps developers get the most out of Nvidia GPUs, reducing training time and costs. These tools give Nvidia an edge because they make its chips more user-friendly.

Over the years, Nvidia has built an entire ecosystem around CUDA. This includes libraries, developer support, and hardware compatibility. The result is that Nvidia's chips are powerful and easier to use than competitors' offerings.

Nvidia's dominance in AI hardware is not just about making fast chips. The company has built an entire system that supports AI development. The H100 GPU remains the top choice for AI training because of its speed and efficiency. The upcoming Blackwell chip promises even better performance, reinforcing Nvidia's lead.

Competitors struggle because Nvidia controls both hardware and software. CUDA locks developers into Nvidia's ecosystem, making it difficult to switch. While other companies try to break into the market, Nvidia's deep integration across AI research, cloud computing, and machine learning gives it a decisive advantage.

CHAPTER 8

THE AI ARMS RACE—
RIVALS, REGULATIONS, AND
GEOPOLITICAL FACTORS

Nvidia has been the leader in AI hardware for years, but competition is growing. Companies like AMD, Intel, and Google are developing AI chips. At the same time, political tensions between the US and China are affecting Nvidia's ability to sell its products worldwide. Governments are also paying closer attention to Nvidia's power in the AI industry. Regulations and policies could change how AI chips are made, sold, and used in the future.

THE RISE OF AI CHIP COMPETITORS: AMD, INTEL, AND GOOGLE'S TPUS

For a long time, Nvidia had little competition in AI hardware. Its GPUs were the best at handling the large amounts of data needed for machine learning. Now, other companies are trying to challenge its dominance.

AMD's Push into AI

AMD has been Nvidia's biggest competitor in gaming GPUs for years.   More recently, it started making AI-focused chips to compete with Nvidia. AMD's MI300X, released in late 2023, is designed for AI training and inference. It uses advanced memory technology to handle large AI models efficiently. Some companies, including Microsoft, have tested AMD's chips as an alternative to Nvidia's.

However, Nvidia still holds an advantage. Most AI developers use software built for Nvidia's CUDA platform. AMD has created ROCm, a software platform similar to CUDA, but it is not as widely used. Many AI researchers and companies hesitate to switch because their existing code runs best on Nvidia hardware.

Intel's Attempt to Enter the AI Market

Once the biggest name in computer processors, Intel has struggled to compete with Nvidia in AI. The company has made several attempts to break into the AI chip market with its Gaudi processors. Intel claims that its Gaudi 3, set to launch in 2024, will offer better price-to-performance than Nvidia's H100 GPU. Some cloud providers, like AWS, have experimented with Intel's AI chips, but they are not yet widely adopted.

Intel faces the same problem as AMD—developers are used to working with Nvidia's software. Even if Intel's hardware is good, convincing AI companies to switch is difficult.

Google's Tensor Processing Units (TPUs)

Google has taken a different approach. Instead of making GPUs, it created TPUs (Tensor Processing Units). These are specialized chips built to run AI models quickly and efficiently. Google has used TPUs for years to power its own AI services, like Google Search and Google Photos.

Unlike AMD and Intel, Google does not sell TPUs as physical chips. Instead, it offers access to TPUs through its Google Cloud Platform. Companies can rent computing power on Google's cloud instead of buying expensive hardware.

TPUs perform well for specific AI tasks but are not as flexible as Nvidia's GPUs. Because Nvidia's chips support a greater variety of software and tools, many AI researchers prefer them.

Why Nvidia Still Holds the Lead

Despite these competitors, Nvidia remains the top choice for AI hardware. The main reasons are:

1. **CUDA Software** – AI developers have spent years building programs that run on Nvidia's platform. Switching to a different system would require rewriting code, which is expensive and time-consuming.

2. **Hardware and Performance** – Nvidia's GPUs, like the H100, offer the best speed, efficiency, and memory capacity for AI training.

3. **Strong Partnerships** – Major cloud providers, including AWS, Microsoft Azure, and Google Cloud, offer Nvidia chips because they are in high demand.

Unless a competitor can match Nvidia's hardware and software ecosystem, the company will likely stay on top.

THE IMPACT OF US-CHINA TECH TENSIONS ON NVIDIA'S GLOBAL EXPANSION

Nvidia is an American company, but its business depends on the global market. Many of its biggest customers, including AI firms and cloud providers, operate worldwide. However, political tensions between the United States and China have made it harder for Nvidia to sell its most advanced chips overseas.

US Export Restrictions on AI Chips

The US government is concerned that China could use advanced AI chips to develop military technology. To prevent this, it has restricted companies like Nvidia, stopping them from selling high-performance AI chips to Chinese customers.

In 2022, the US government banned Nvidia from selling its A100 and H100 GPUs to China. In response, Nvidia created weaker versions of these chips, called the A800 and H800, specifically for the Chinese market. However, in 2023, the US tightened its rules again, blocking even these modified chips.

These restrictions have hurt Nvidia's business in China. Before the bans, Chinese tech companies, including Alibaba, Tencent, and Baidu, were major buyers of Nvidia's chips. Without access to Nvidia's best hardware, these companies must look for alternatives. Some are now turning to domestic chipmakers like Huawei, which is working on its own AI chips.

How China is Responding

China does not want to depend on American technology for AI development. In recent years, the Chinese government has made significant investments in domestic chip manufacturing. Companies like SMIC (Semiconductor Manufacturing International Corporation) and Huawei are trying to build AI chips that compete with Nvidia's.

However, China still faces significant challenges. The most advanced AI chips require cutting-edge manufacturing techniques; which China does not yet have. For now, Nvidia's GPUs remain the best option for training AI, even if they are harder to obtain.

The Future of US-China AI Competition

The rivalry between the US and China is unlikely to end soon. The US wants to keep its lead in AI technology, while China is determined to catch up. Nvidia will have to navigate these challenges carefully. If tensions continue, Nvidia may lose more of its Chinese customers. At the same time, US restrictions could slow global AI development by making it harder for companies to access the best hardware.

REGULATORY SCRUTINY ON NVIDIA'S MARKET POWER AND AI'S ETHICAL CONCERNS

As Nvidia's influence grows, governments are paying more attention. Some regulators worry that Nvidia controls the AI hardware market too much. Others are concerned about the ethical risks of AI and want stricter rules on how AI chips are used.

Concerns About Nvidia's Market Power

Nvidia is the clear leader in AI chips, but some see this as a problem. Critics argue that:

- Nvidia's dominance makes AI development too dependent on one company.
- High demand for Nvidia chips has increased prices, making AI research more expensive.
- The company's close partnerships with cloud providers could limit competition.

In 2022, Nvidia attempted to buy Arm, a British company that designs processor technology. Regulators blocked the deal, fearing it would give Nvidia too much control over the semiconductor industry. Since then, Nvidia has faced more scrutiny over its market power.

Ethical Concerns About AI and Nvidia's Role

AI can be used for many good things, but also has risks. Governments worry that powerful AI models could:

- Spread misinformation by generating fake images, videos, or articles.
- Replace human jobs, especially in industries like customer service and content creation.
- Be misused for surveillance, hacking, or automated weapons.

Because Nvidia provides the chips that power AI models, some believe the company should take more responsibility for how its technology is used. Regulators may introduce new rules requiring AI chipmakers to ensure ethical AI development.

HOW GOVERNMENT POLICIES COULD SHAPE THE FUTURE OF AI CHIP DEVELOPMENT

AI is growing rapidly, and governments are trying to keep up. The policies they create will significantly impact companies like Nvidia, AMD, and Intel.

Possible Future Regulations

Governments may introduce rules to:

- **Limit AI chip exports** to certain countries for security reasons.
- **AI chipmakers must track how their hardware** is used to prevent misuse.
- **Encourage competition** by supporting new AI chip companies.
- **Set energy efficiency standards** for AI data centers.

Some countries also invest in domestic AI chip production to reduce reliance on Nvidia and other US firms. The European Union, for example, has announced funding to support AI chip research in Europe.

How Nvidia and Its Rivals Will Respond

Nvidia will need to adapt to changing regulations. If governments push for more competition, Nvidia may face new rivals. If restrictions on AI chip exports continue, Nvidia could lose access to important markets.

At the same time, demand for AI chips is not slowing down. Nvidia's future will depend on how well it can balance innovation, competition, and government policies in the coming years.

CHAPTER 9

NVIDIA'S LONG-TERM STRATEGY AND THE FUTURE OF AI

Nvidia is at the core of the rapidly expanding field of artificial intelligence. Over the next ten years, AI will play a more significant role in daily life, transforming sectors like robotics, healthcare, and quantum computing. Nvidia knows that maintaining its lead in AI requires more than producing superior GPUs. The company's long-term goals include entering new markets, extending AI beyond cloud computing, and maintaining its position as the leading AI software and hardware manufacturer.

THE NEXT DECADE ROADMAP FROM NVIDIA

For many years, Nvidia has dominated the AI hardware market and has no intention of slowing down. The business is investing in new technologies to maintain its edge in AI computing. Nvidia is concentrating on the following areas:

1. Stronger AI Chips

Nvidia frequently releases new GPUs that push the boundaries of AI performance. The 2023 release of the H100 chip marked a significant advancement in AI training capabilities. It is anticipated that Nvidia's upcoming major chip, Blackwell, will further enhance performance. Nvidia will continue to release increasingly potent chips every few years.

2. Better AI Software

One of Nvidia's most significant advantages is its CUDA software. Due to CUDA's hardware optimization, developers use it to create AI models. To make its AI software tools even more user-friendly, the company is expanding them and refining CUDA.

3. Training for Energy-Efficient AI Computing

AI models requires a significant amount of electricity. Nvidia is developing AI chips that are more energy-efficient without sacrificing performance. This will lower costs for businesses utilizing Nvidia's hardware and make AI more sustainable.

4. AI-Powered Supercomputers

Additionally, Nvidia is developing supercomputers with AI in mind. These potent devices will assist researchers in areas such as materials science, climate science, and medicine in resolving challenging issues.

With these developments, Nvidia intends to maintain its position as the leading option for AI computing in the upcoming years.

INCREASING AI'S POTENTIAL OUTSIDE OF CLOUD COMPUTING

The majority of AI is currently used in cloud data centers. Google, Microsoft, and Amazon use Nvidia chips to power AI models in large server farms. However, AI is making it into everyday devices and beyond the cloud. Nvidia is developing edge computing AI hardware, which enables AI to operate locally on devices rather than relying on remote data centers.

AI at the Edge

Edge computing improves speed and lessens dependency on internet connections by bringing AI closer to the user. Nvidia is creating edge AI chips that apply to:

- **Smartphones and tablets** – AI-powered features like voice assistants and real-time translation work better when processed directly on a device.

- **AI-powered security cameras** don't require a continuous cloud connection to identify suspicious activity and issue alerts.

- **Drones** with autonomous AI capabilities can assess their environment and make snap decisions without transmitting information to a server.

- **Industrial automation:** AI at the edge can be used in factories and warehouses for robotic management and real-time quality control.

AI in Self-Driving Cars

AI for autonomous vehicles is one of Nvidia's most ambitious initiatives. The company's Drive platform supplies the computing power required for autonomous vehicles. These AI systems analyze lidar sensors, radar, and camera data to make driving decisions.

According to Nvidia, most cars on the road will be powered by AI. According to Jensen Huang, the company's CEO, every car will eventually become a "robot on wheels." To make this a reality, Nvidia is collaborating with automakers like Tesla, Mercedes-Benz, and Toyota to create cutting-edge driver-assistance technologies.

REACHING NEW MARKETS IN ROBOTICS, QUANTUM COMPUTING, AND HEALTHCARE

AI isn't limited to self-driving cars and cloud computing. Nvidia is branching into new fields where AI can make a significant difference.

AI in Medical Fields

AI is utilized in healthcare to speed up diagnosis, perso nalize treatment, and find new drugs. Nvidia is creating AI-driven technologies that can evaluate medical images, identify illnesses sooner, and assist physicians in choosing the best course of action.

For instance, using artificial intelligence, Nvidia's Clara platform processes medical scans, such as CT and MRI scans. AI can draw attention to problem areas, assisting medical professionals in identifying issues that the human eye might overlook.

AI is also being utilized to create new medications. Pharmaceutical companies use Nvidia's AI systems to model the effects of drugs on the human body, expediting the development of novel therapies.

Robotics Driven by AI

AI-powered robots are increasingly being used in homes, businesses, and warehouses. Nvidia's Isaac platform provides the hardware and software required to train AI robots. These robots are capable of:

- Help with warehouse duties like sorting and packaging.
- Assist surgeons with exacting medical treatments.
- Do housework, such as mowing the lawn and vacuuming.

As AI advances, robots will perform increasingly difficult tasks. Thanks to its investment in robotics, Nvidia is positioned to gain from this expansion.

AI and Quantum Computing

Although it is still in its infancy, quantum computing has the potential to transform artificial intelligence completely. Unlike conventional computers, quantum computers use qubits, which can exist in multiple states at once. which process information in binary (0s and 1s). Because of this, they can solve issues far more quickly than traditional computers.

Nvidia is investigating methods to integrate quantum computing and artificial intelligence. The aim is creating models that assists in developing novel materials or finding new medications. Although it will be years before any practical quantum computers are developed, Nvidia is establishing itself as a pioneer in this new area.

AI'S IMPACT ON REVOLUTIONIZING DAILY LIFE AND INDUSTRIES

AI is already altering how people use technology and how businesses run. Over the next ten years, AI will be further incorporated into daily life.

AI in Business

Businesses are using AI to increase productivity and decision-making. AI-powered chatbots handle customer service, AI-driven software aids data analysis, and AI assistants increase employee productivity. At the core of this change are Nvidia's software and hardware.

AI in Education

Colleges and universities are using AI to customize instruction. AI tutors can modify lessons based on a student's development. Assignments can receive immediate feedback from AI grading systems. These educational apps are powered in part by Nvidia's AI tools.

AI in Entertainment

AI is being creatively used in video games, music, and movies. It is capable of producing lifelike digital characters, enhancing the visuals in video games, and even producing music. Thanks to Nvidia's Omniverse platform, developers and artists can use AI in novel and exciting ways.

Smart Home AI

Smart home appliances already use AI and answer questions from Google Assistant and Amazon Alexa. AI may eventually be able to control every aspect of a house, including the temperature, lighting, and security, according to user preferences. Many of these smart home innovations will be powered by Nvidia's AI chips.

FORECASTS FOR THE DEVELOPMENT OF AI AND NVIDIA'S STRATEGIES FOR STAYING AHEAD

AI is predicted to expand quickly over the next ten years. As more businesses invest in AI-powered solutions, the industry will grow to be worth trillions of dollars, according to experts.

Access to AI Will Increase

Large tech firms and research institutes are currently the primary users of AI. AI will eventually be more widely available to individuals and small enterprises. To enable anyone to create and use AI models, Nvidia is creating user-friendly AI tools.

AI Will Power More Devices

AI is expanding beyond smartphones and PCs. Within the next ten years, AI will be incorporated into automobiles, home appliances, and even wearable technology. AI chips from Nvidia will be essential to this growth.

Regulation of AI Will Rise

As AI gains strength, governments will enact more regulations. As it continues to innovate, Nvidia will need to collaborate with legislators to guarantee that AI is used responsibly.

AI Hardware Will Continue to Be Led by Nvidia

Despite escalating competition, Nvidia is in a strong position to maintain its lead in AI computing. The company has a significant edge because of its emphasis on software, hardware, and AI research. Nvidia's impact will only increase as AI spreads into new sectors.

CONCLUSION

NVIDIA'S FUTURE AND THE UNSTOPPABLE POWER OF AI

Artificial intelligence has already influenced businesses, industries, and daily life. It is no longer merely a futuristic idea. A major contributor to this change has been Nvidia. The company's powerful GPUs have emerged as the foundation of AI, driving developments in robotics, cloud computing, medical research, and self-driving cars. Nvidia finds itself at a turning point as AI keeps growing. Will a new rival emerge to challenge its position, or will it continue to dominate?

THE FINANCIAL SUCCESS OF NVIDIA IN 2024 AND ITS CONSEQUENCES

In 2024, Nvidia's financial results were nothing short of remarkable. The business's annual profits more than doubled to $74.3 billion. Demand for AI chips was a significant factor in the 78% increase in sales. These figures are remarkable, and they also demonstrate that Nvidia is currently the leading manufacturer of AI hardware.

The company's power goes beyond its financial achievements. Nvidia has established itself as a gauge for the artificial intelligence sector. The whole AI industry gains when Nvidia does well. The stock prices of tech giants like Google, Meta, Microsoft, and Amazon increased following the release of the company's earnings report. This demonstrates Nvidia's close ties to the more significant AI industry.

Even with this financial success, there are still some issues. Investors are concerned about new AI models that could increase AI's efficiency without depending as heavily on Nvidia's chips and competition from firms like AMD, Intel, and Google. Government regulations and geopolitical tensions between the United States and China may also affect Nvidia's capacity to sustain its current momentum.

THE HARMONY OF MARKET DOMINANCE, INNOVATION, AND COMPETITION

Due to its success, Nvidia is now a target for rivals. Other businesses are rushing to create their own AI chips to overtake Nvidia as the market leader.

- **AMD** has unveiled AI-focused GPUs in an effort to compete with Nvidia's H100 and the impending **Blackwell** chips.

- **Intel** is making headway with its **Gaudi AI chips**, which promise powerful performance at a reduced price.

- **Tensor Processing Units (TPUs)**, which are specially made for AI workloads and tailored for **Google's** services, have been the subject of significant Google investments.

Even though these businesses are improving, Nvidia has a significant edge. It has spent years improving both its software ecosystem and hardware. Since many AI models are designed to run on the CUDA platform, Nvidia has an advantage. Nvidia stays ahead of the competition because switching to a competitor's hardware is difficult.

However, constant innovation is necessary to maintain dominance. With the speed at which technology is developing, Nvidia cannot afford to slow down. The business must keep enhancing its chips, cutting energy use, and breaking into new markets. Growing worries about AI's effects on ethics, security, and employment must also be addressed.

WILL A NEW PLAYER ENTER THE AI REVOLUTION, OR WILL NVIDIA CONTINUE TO LEAD?

As history demonstrates, even the largest businesses can be disrupted. Intel used to be the market leader in computer processors, but AMD and Apple's M-series chips have since seized a sizable portion of the market. Microsoft used to dominate the smartphone operating system market, but Apple's iOS and Google's Android swept it away.

Would Nvidia experience the same fate?

A few situations could put Nvidia's supremacy in jeopardy:

1. A New Development in AI Chips

The most powerful chips for AI at the moment are Nvidia's GPUs. However, Nvidia's position might deteriorate if a business creates a new kind of AI processor that is more affordable and effective. Google's TPUs have already shown promise, and other businesses might do the same.

2. AI Models Become More Efficient

The demand for Nvidia's high-performance GPUs may decline if AI companies learn how to train and operate AI models with less processing power. A Chinese AI model called DeepSeek has already demonstrated that certain AI systems can operate more effectively. If this trend continues, businesses might not require as many Nvidia chips.

3. Geopolitical and Regulatory Challenges

Due to concerns about AI and national security, the U.S. government has already restricted Nvidia's ability to sell advanced chips to China. If more nations impose similar regulations, Nvidia may lose access to important markets. Governments may also impose more stringent rules on AI firms, which would impact Nvidia's operations.

4. A Change in Preferences for AI Hardware

Companies like Microsoft, Amazon, and Meta currently use Nvidia's chips for artificial intelligence. However, some of these companies are working on their own custom AI chips to reduce dependence on Nvidia. If they are successful, Nvidia may lose some of its largest clients.

Despite these risks, Nvidia is not standing still. Even if AI technology changes, the company is actively branching out into new fields to remain relevant.

CONCLUDING REMARKS ON AI'S FUTURE AND NVIDIA'S CONTRIBUTION

The growth of AI is astounding. Industries are already being altered by it, and its influence will only grow in the years to come. With its software and hardware that drive AI systems, Nvidia is at the forefront of this change. However, the business must remain ahead of obstacles like competition, laws, and technological changes.

AI's Future

AI will grow even more potent and pervasive over the next ten years. Here are some examples of how AI will influence the future:

- **AI-powered healthcare** will assist physicians in developing individualized treatments and making earlier disease diagnoses.
- **AI-driven automation** will change industries, from manufacturing to customer service.
- **Self-driving cars** will become more common, improving transportation safety and efficiency.
- AI will aid writing, music composition, and even filmmaking in **creative industries**.

- **AI assistants** will become more competent, helping people with daily tasks in more natural ways.

Many of these developments will be powered by Nvidia's chips. The company invests in robotics, quantum computing, supercomputers, and AI research to stay on the cutting edge of AI technology.

Will Nvidia Continue to Lead?

The next few years will be crucial for Nvidia. The company must continue pushing the limits of AI hardware while expanding into new industries. It also needs to prepare for more government rules and competition from tech companies.

Despite the difficulties, Nvidia has several significant advantages:

- **Nvidia already dominates AI hardware.** Most AI businesses use Nvidia's GPUs, and switching to a different supplier can be challenging.

- **Its software ecosystem is unmatched**—CUDA and Nvidia's AI development tools make it easier for businesses to stick with Nvidia hardware.
- **It is entering new markets.** Nvidia is securing its future beyond GPUs by investing in robotics, healthcare, and quantum computing.

Conclusion Nvidia has proven itself as the leader in AI computing, and its success in 2024 shows the demand for its technology is stronger than ever. It won't be simple to stay at the top, though. Governments are tightening regulations, rivals are creating AI chips, and AI technology is evolving quickly.

However, Nvidia is still in a strong position to dominate the AI market. Thanks to its potent hardware, robust software, and ongoing innovation, it has a significant edge. Nvidia will continue to impact AI for years to come, even though new competitors may join the market.

The AI revolution is unstoppable; for now, Nvidia is leading the charge.